# My Father Is a Teacher Overseas

Piper Nelid

Rosen REAL READERS

Rosen Classroom™
New York

My father is a teacher.

He teaches overseas.

My father teaches English
in China.
He has a class full of students.

I go to school with my father.

I am not one of his students.

I am learning other subjects.

His students learn how to speak
and read English.
Sometimes they go to the library.

The library has many books. Some are in English. These books will help my father's students.

My father teaches his students new words every day.

Today, they are learning about American sports.

My father's favorite sport is football.
He enjoys teaching his students the rules.

Football players wear helmets. They also wear a lot of padding. Padding is used to keep the players safe.

He teaches his students what
a football looks like.
The ball is made from rubber.
He shows how this helps a
player hold the ball.

My father is a great teacher.
His students love learning about football.
They are now learning how to play.

# Words to Know

football

helmet

library

students